IT IT IT
MUST MUST MUST MU
BE BE B
OVE LO LO

IT IT IT
MUST MUST MUST
BE BE BE
LOVE LOVE LOVE L

IT IT IT
MUST MUST MUST MU
BE BE BE B
OVE LOVE LOVE LO

IT IT IT
MUST MUST MUST
BE BE BE
LOVE LOVE LOVE L

IT IT IT IT
MUST MUST MUST MUST
BE BE BE BE
LOVE LOVE LOVE LOVE

IT IT IT
MUST MUST MUST MU
BE BE BE B
OVE LOVE LOVE LO

IT IT IT IT
MUST MUST MUST MUS
BE BE BE BE
VE LOVE LOVE LOVE

IT IT IT
MUST MUST MUST MU
BE BE BE B
OVE LOVE LOVE LO

14/2/16

IT
MUST
BE
LOVE

Yours
Olive
xxoo

IT MUST BE LOVE

Summersdale Publishers Ltd
46 West Street
Chichester
West Sussex
PO19 1RP
UK

www.summersdale.com

Printed and bound in the Czech Republic

ISBN: 978-1-84953-206-8

Substantial discounts on bulk quantities of Summersdale books are available to corporations, professional associations and other organisations. For details telephone Summersdale Publishers on (+44-1243-771107), fax (+44-1243-786300) or email (nicky@summersdale.com).

IT
MUST
BE
LOVE

summersdale

Where there is
great love, there are
always miracles.

Willa Cather

A kiss makes the heart
young again and wipes out
the years.

Rupert Brooke

I love her and that's
the beginning of
everything.

F. Scott Fitzgerald

I love you not because of
who you are, but because of
who I am when I am
with you.

Roy Croft

Love is never lost. If not reciprocated, it will flow back and soften and purify the heart.

Washington Irving

If you press me to say why
I loved him, I can say no
more than because he was
he, and I was I.

Michel de Montaigne

I don't smoke, I don't drink
to excess, but I've always
loved women. I don't see
that as a vice.

Tom Conti

Love is being stupid together.

Paul Valéry

No job is as important to me
as my love.

Jennifer Aniston

My sort of religion is
one of romance.

Christopher Plummer

In the arithmetic of
love, one plus one
equals everything,
and two minus one
equals nothing.

Mignon McLaughlin

I want to be with my best friend, and my best friend's my wife. Who could ask for anything more?

John Lennon

Looking back, I have this to regret, that too often when I loved, I did not say so.

David Grayson

Being deeply loved by someone gives you strength, while loving someone deeply gives you courage.

Lao Tzu

Love is only a dirty trick
played on us to achieve
continuation of the species.

W. Somerset Maugham

Love me when I least
deserve it, because
that's when I really
need it.

Swedish proverb

But to see her was to love
her, love but her, and
love forever.

Robert Burns

Who, being loved, is poor?

Oscar Wilde

Flying.

Julia Donaldson describing what love feels like

In doing something, do it
with love or never do
it at all.

Mahatma Gandhi

You know it's love when…
He holds your hair back
when you're being sick after
a big night out.

Clare Grogan

Love takes off masks
that we fear we cannot
live without and know
we cannot live within.

James Baldwin

I knew that I wanted to marry her after the first day I met her.

Tom Cruise on Katie Holmes

Love is an emotion
experienced by the many
and enjoyed by the few.

George Jean Nathan

I can live without
money, but I cannot
live without love.

Judy Garland

Love doesn't just sit there,
like a stone, it has to be
made, like bread; re-made
all the time.

Ursula K. Le Guin

It was a bolt of
lightning to the heart.

Colin Firth on seeing his wife
Livia for the first time

Gravitation is not
responsible for people
falling in love.

Albert Einstein

The hunger for love
is much more difficult
to remove than the
hunger for bread.

Mother Teresa

Love is the self-delusion we
manufacture to justify the
trouble we take to have sex.

Daniel S. Greenberg

The best smell in the world is that man that you love.

Jennifer Aniston

A kiss is a lovely trick
designed by nature to
stop speech when words
become superfluous.

Ingrid Bergman

The most powerful
weapon on earth is
the human soul
on fire.

Ferdinand Foch

Before I met my husband, I'd never fallen in love. I'd stepped in it a few times.

Rita Rudner

Love is an act of endless
forgiveness, a tender look
which becomes a habit.

Peter Ustinov

I think beauty comes
from being happy
and connected to the
people we love.

Marcia Cross

Love is the hardest habit to break, and the most difficult to satisfy.

Drew Barrymore

Love in its essence is
spiritual fire.

Emanuel Swedenborg

Why love if losing hurts so
much? We love to know that
we are not alone.

C. S. Lewis

The good life is
inspired by love and
guided by knowledge.

Bertrand Russell

Eskimos had fifty-two names
for snow because it was
important to them: there
ought to be as many
for love.

Margaret Atwood

The opposite of
loneliness... it's not
togetherness. It
is intimacy.

Richard Bach

… my love for Heathcliff
resembles the eternal rocks
beneath – a source of
little visible delight,
but necessary.

Emily Brontë, *Wuthering Heights*

The love we give
away is the only love
we keep.

Elbert Hubbard

True love stories
never have endings.

Richard Bach

Thus love has the
magic power to make of a
beggar a king. Yes, love is
free; it can dwell in no
other atmosphere.

Emma Goldman

We need not think
alike to love alike.

Ferenc Dávid

The giving of love is an
education in itself.

Eleanor Roosevelt

My wife picked me out of a soccer sticker book. And I chose her off the telly...

David Beckham on
Victoria Beckham

Love at first sight is probably
a myth, but profound and
mutual attraction can grow
into love.

Trudie Styler

A wild plant that, when it blooms by chance within the hedge of our gardens, we call a flower; and when it blooms outside we call a weed; but, flower or weed, whose scent and colour are always, wild!

John Galsworthy on love,
The Forsyte Saga

Love is composed of a single soul inhabiting two bodies.

Aristotle

What the world really
needs is more love
and less paperwork.

Pearl Bailey

Love is that condition in
which the happiness of
another person is essential
to your own.

Robert A. Heinlein

What a happy and holy fashion it is that those who love one another should rest on the same pillow.

Nathaniel Hawthorne

Sex is a part of
nature. I go along
with nature.

Marilyn Monroe

When one has once fully
entered the realm of love,
the world – no matter how
imperfect – becomes rich
and beautiful, it consists
solely of opportunities
for love.

Søren Kierkegaard

Love has no
uttermost, as the stars
have no number and
the sea no rest.

Eleanor Farjeon

We come to love not by
finding the perfect person,
but by learning to see an
imperfect person perfectly.

Sam Keen

Love life and life will love you back. Love people and they will love you back.

Arthur Rubinstein

Yet the light of a
whole life dies
When love is done.

Francis William Bourdillon, from
'The Night has a Thousand Eyes'

The one thing we can never
get enough of… and… give
enough of is love.

Henry Miller

Love makes your soul crawl
out from its hiding place.

Zora Neale Hurston

The first duty of love is to listen.

Paul Tillich

Love… isn't sentimental. It doesn't have to be pretty, yet it doesn't deny pain.

Sharon Salzberg

Nothing we do, however
virtuous, can be
accomplished alone;
therefore, we are saved
by love.

Reinhold Niebuhr

Love is the axis and breath of my life. The art I produce is a byproduct.

Anaïs Nin

We're all going to die, all of us, what a circus! That alone should make us love each other.

Charles Bukowski

When you're comfortable
with someone you love, the
silence is the best.

Britney Spears

Love is a better teacher than duty.

Albert Einstein

Experience is how life
catches up with us and
teaches us to love and
forgive each other.

Judy Collins

Be loving, and you will
never want for love;
be humble, and you
will never want
for guiding.

Dinah Craik

The most important thing in
life is to learn how to give
out love, and to let it
come in.

Morrie Schwartz

A career is wonderful,
but you can't curl up
with it on a cold night.

Marilyn Monroe

If I know what love is,
it is because of you.

Hermann Hesse

Where love rules, there is
no will to power; and where
power predominates, there
love is lacking.

Carl Jung

Love is the magician
that pulls man out of
his own hat.

Ben Hecht

Let the lover be disgraceful,
crazy, absent-minded.
Someone sober will worry
about events going badly.
Let the lover be.

Rumi

Take away love and
our earth is a tomb.

Robert Browning

Love is a game that two can play and both win.

Eva Gabor

Age does not protect you
from love. But love, to some
extent, protects you
from age.

Jeanne Moreau

The best love
affairs are those we
never had.

Norman Lindsay

Power without love is
reckless and abusive,
and love without power is
sentimental and anaemic.

Martin Luther King Jr

I kissed a lot of frogs
and now I've found
my prince.

Joan Collins

Love doesn't make the world go round. Love is what makes the ride worthwhile.

Franklin P. Jones

We are the leaves of one
branch, the drops of one
sea, the flowers of
one garden.

Jean-Baptiste Henri Lacordaire

A purpose of human life, no
matter who is controlling it,
is to love whoever is around
to be loved.

Kurt Vonnegut Jr

What does love feel like? Incredible.

Rebecca Adlington

For one human being to
love another: that is perhaps
the most difficult of our
tasks, the ultimate, the last
test and proof, the work for
which all other work is
but preparation.

Rainer Maria Rilke

Love knows not
distance; it hath no
continent; its eyes are
for the stars…

Gilbert Parker

The winds were warm about us, the whole earth seemed the wealthier for our love.

Harriet Prescott Spofford,
The Amber Gods

Women are meant
to be loved, not to
be understood.

Oscar Wilde

There is no
happiness in love,
except at the end of
an English novel.

Anthony Trollope

Love cures people – both
the ones who give it and the
ones who receive it.

Karl Menninger

It was not my lips you
kissed, but my soul.

Judy Garland

Love is friendship set on fire.

Jeremy Taylor

Such young unfurrowed
souls roll to meet each other
like two velvet peaches that
touch softly and are
at rest...

George Eliot, *Adam Bede*

That's the nature, the
meaning, the best of
life itself.

Zane Grey on love

You know it's love when…
After fourteen years
together you still get
butterflies in your stomach
when you see someone.

Antony Worrall Thompson

(You LoVE
oL

What is hell?
I maintain that it is
the suffering of being
unable to love.

Fyodor Dostoevsky

Love is a great
beautifier.

Louisa May Alcott

But love is omniembracing, omnicoherent, and omni-inclusive, *with no exceptions*. Love, like synergetics, is nondifferentiable, i.e., is integral.

R. Buckminster Fuller

Love involves a peculiar
unfathomable combination
of understanding and
misunderstanding.

Diane Arbus

Forgiveness is
choosing to love.
It is the first skill of
self-giving love.

Mahatma Gandhi

Love, whether newly-born
or aroused from a death-like
slumber, must always create
sunshine, filling the hearts
so full of radiance, that
it overflows upon the
outward world.

Nathaniel Hawthorne

You are my heart, my life, my one and only thought.

Sir Arthur Conan Doyle

All love shifts and changes.
I don't know if you can be
wholeheartedly in love all
the time.

Julie Andrews

I don't want to live. I
want to love first, and
live incidentally.

Zelda Fitzgerald

Love loves to
love love.

James Joyce

Reason is nothing less than
the guardian of love.

Sam Harris

Did my heart love till now?
Forswear it, sight.
For I ne'er saw true beauty
till this night.

William Shakespeare,
Romeo and Juliet

Love is the only bow
on Life's dark cloud.

Robert G. Ingersoll

Life isn't long enough for love and art.

W. Somerset Maugham

Love is like pi – natural,
irrational, and very
important.

Lisa Hoffman

The madness of love
is the greatest of
heaven's blessings.

Plato

Love, it is said, is blind, but love is not blind. It is an extra eye, which shows us what is most worthy of regard.

James M. Barrie, *The Little Minister*

Tell me whom you
love and I will tell you
who you are.

Arsène Houssaye

Love, you know, seeks to
make happy rather than to
be happy.

Ralph Connor

To say 'I love you' one must
first be able to say the 'I'.

Ayn Rand

Love is in all things
a most wonderful
teacher...

Charles Dickens, *Our Mutual Friend*

Never begrudge your
partner's passion.

Louise Redknapp

Love is a growing, or full
constant light;
And his first minute, after
noon, is night.

John Donne

Time is too slow for those
who wait, too swift for those
who fear, too long for those
who grieve, too short for
those who rejoice, but for
those who love, time
is eternity.

Henry van Dyke

She is the heart
that strikes a whole
octave. After her all
songs are possible.

Rainer Maria Rilke

Just because someone doesn't love you the way you want them to, doesn't mean they don't love you.

Truman Capote

Love gives naught but
itself and takes naught
but from itself.

Khalil Gibran

I see that I was mistaken
about Eve in the beginning;
it is better to live outside the
Garden with her than inside
it without her.

Mark Twain

It is perhaps the
only glimpse we are
permitted of eternity.

Helen Hayes on love

The world is too dangerous for anything but truth and too small for anything but love.

William Sloane Coffin

The most wonderful of all things in life is the discovery of another human being with whom one's relationship has a growing depth, beauty and joy as the years increase.

Sir Hugh Walpole

We can only learn to
love by loving.

Iris Murdoch

Love does not consist of gazing at each other, but in looking together in the same direction.

Antoine de Saint-Exupéry

'We are all born for love,' said Morley. 'It is the principle of existence, and its only end.'

Benjamin Disraeli, *Sybil*

Love is everything it's cracked up to be… worth fighting for, being brave for, risking everything for.

Erica Jong

Woe to the man whose
heart has not learned while
young to hope, to love – and
to put its trust in life.

Joseph Conrad

Love must be as much
a light as it is a flame.

Henry David Thoreau

We don't believe in
rheumatism and true
love until after the
first attack.

Marie E. Eschenbach

… love from one being to another can only be that two solitudes come nearer, recognise and protect and comfort each other.

Han Suyin

All mankind love a lover.

Ralph Waldo Emerson

Talk not of wasted affection;
affection never was wasted.

Henry Wadsworth Longfellow

Love is what is left in a relationship after all the selfishness has been removed.

Cullen Hightower

Each time that one loves is
the only time one has ever
loved. Difference of object
does not alter singleness
of passion. It merely
intensifies it.

Oscar Wilde

We can live without religion
and meditation, but we
cannot survive without
human affection.

Tenzin Gyatso, 14th Dalai Lama

Love does not alter
the beloved, it
alters itself.

Søren Kierkegaard

Those who love deeply
never grow old; they may
die of old age, but they
die young.

Arthur Wing Pinero

The highest form of
affection is based on
full sincerity on
both sides.

Thomas Hardy, *Jude the Obscure*

The ultimate lesson all
of us have to learn is
unconditional love, which
includes not only others
but ourselves.

Elisabeth Kübler-Ross

Love is the enchanted
dawn of every heart.

Alphonse Marie de la Martine

In dreams and in love there are no impossibilities.

Janos Arnay

Eventually you will come to understand that love heals everything, and love is all there is.

Gary Zukav

When the heart speaks,
however simple the words,
its language is always
acceptable to those who
have hearts.

Mary Baker Eddy

There is no remedy for love but to love more.

Henry David Thoreau

[He is] quite simply my strength and stay.

The Queen on Prince Philip

Everything in our life should
be based on love.

Ray Bradbury

ALL YOU NEED IS LOVE

£4.99

ISBN: 978 1 84953 130 6

*'Love is an irresistible desire
to be irresistibly desired.'*

Robert Frost

HEARTFELT WORDS FOR STARRY-EYED LOVERS

When John Lennon wrote that 'all you need is love' back in 1967, perhaps he'd been struck by the lovebug himself. Love is a gift, love is an adventure, love is a many-splendoured thing – love is what makes the world go round, so why not spread a little of the sweet stuff right now?

Here's a book packed with quotations that will have you feeling the love in no time.

www.summersdale.com

IT
MUST
BE
LOVE

IT
MUST
BE
LOVE

IT
MUST
BE
LOVE

IT
MUST
BE
LOVE

IT MUST BE LOVE IT MUST BE LOVE IT MUST BE LOVE IT MUST BE LOVE

IT MUST BE LOVE IT MUST BE LOVE IT MUST BE LOVE IT MUST BE LOVE

IT MUST BE LOVE IT MUST BE LOVE IT MUST BE LOVE IT MUST BE LOVE

IT MUST BE LOVE IT MUST BE LOVE IT MUST BE LOVE IT MUST BE LOVE